BOOK TWO:

A DOZEN A DAY

*Pre-Practice
Technical Exercises*
FOR THE PIANO

by
Edna-Mae Burnam

© 1950, 1996 The Willis Music Company, Florence, KY, USA
Reproducing this music in any form is illegal and forbidden
by the Copyright, Designs and Patents Act 1988.

Exclusive distributors:
Music Sales Limited, 14/15 Berners Street, London W1T 3LJ.
Music Sales Pty Limited, 20 Resolution Drive, Caringbah, NSW 2229, Australia.

To my family

A DOZEN A DAY

Many people do physical exercises every morning before they go to work.

Likewise— we should all give our fingers exercises every day BEFORE we begin our practising.

The purpose of this book is to help develop strong hands and flexible fingers.

Do not try to learn the entire first dozen exercises the first week you study this book! Just learn two or three exercises and do them each day *before* practising. When these are mastered, add another, then another, and keep adding until the twelve can be played perfectly.

When the first dozen—Group I—have been mastered and perfected—Group II may be introduced in the same manner.

When the entire book is finished, any of the groups may be transposed to different keys. In fact, this should be encouraged.

EDNA-MAE BURNAM

CONTENTS

GROUP I 1
1. Walking and Running
2. Skipping
3. Hopping
4. Deep Breathing
5. Deep Knee Bend
6. Stretching
7. Stretching Right Leg Up
8. Stretching Left Leg
9. Cartwheels
10. The Splits
11. Standing on Head
12. Fit as a Fiddle and Ready to Go

GROUP II 5
1. Morning Stretch
2. Walking
3. Running
4. High Stepping
5. Jumping
6. Kicking Right Leg
7. Kicking Left Leg
8. The Splits
9. Leg Work (*lying down*)
10. Sitting Up and Lying Down
11. A Hard Trick
12. Fit as a Fiddle and Ready to Go

GROUP III 10
1. Deep Breathing
2. Rolling
3. Climbing (*in place*)
4. Tip-toe Running (*in place*)
5. Baby Steps
6. Giant Steps
7. Jumping Rope
8. Somersaults
9. Touching Toes
10. Ballet Exercise (" *Entre chat quatre* ")
11. The Splits
12. Fit as a Fiddle and Ready to Go

GROUP IV 15
1. Morning Stretch
2. Climbing (*in place*)
3. Tip-toe Running (*in place*)
4. Running
5. Cartwheels
6. Touching Toes
7. Hopping
8. Baby Steps
9. Giant Steps
10. Flinging Arms Out and Back
11. Standing on Head
12. Fit as a Fiddle and Ready to Go

GROUP V 21
1. Deep Breathing
2. Touching Toes
3. Hopping
4. Climbing a Ladder
5. Jumping Rope (*Slow, and " Red Pepper* ")
6. Swinging Arms
7. Hand Springs
8. Walking like a Duck
9. Bear Walk
10. Sliding Down the Bannister
11. A Hard Trick
12. Fit as a Fiddle and Ready to Go

Group I
1. Walking and Running

1st time—legato (smooth, connected)
2nd time—staccato (sharp, detached)

2. Skipping

legato—staccato

swing rythm (do be do be)
List fingers before play
stroke sigs toward you

3. Hopping

staccato

Copyright, MCML, by The Willis Music Co.
International Copyright Secured

4. Deep Breathing

5. Deep Knee Bend

6. Stretching

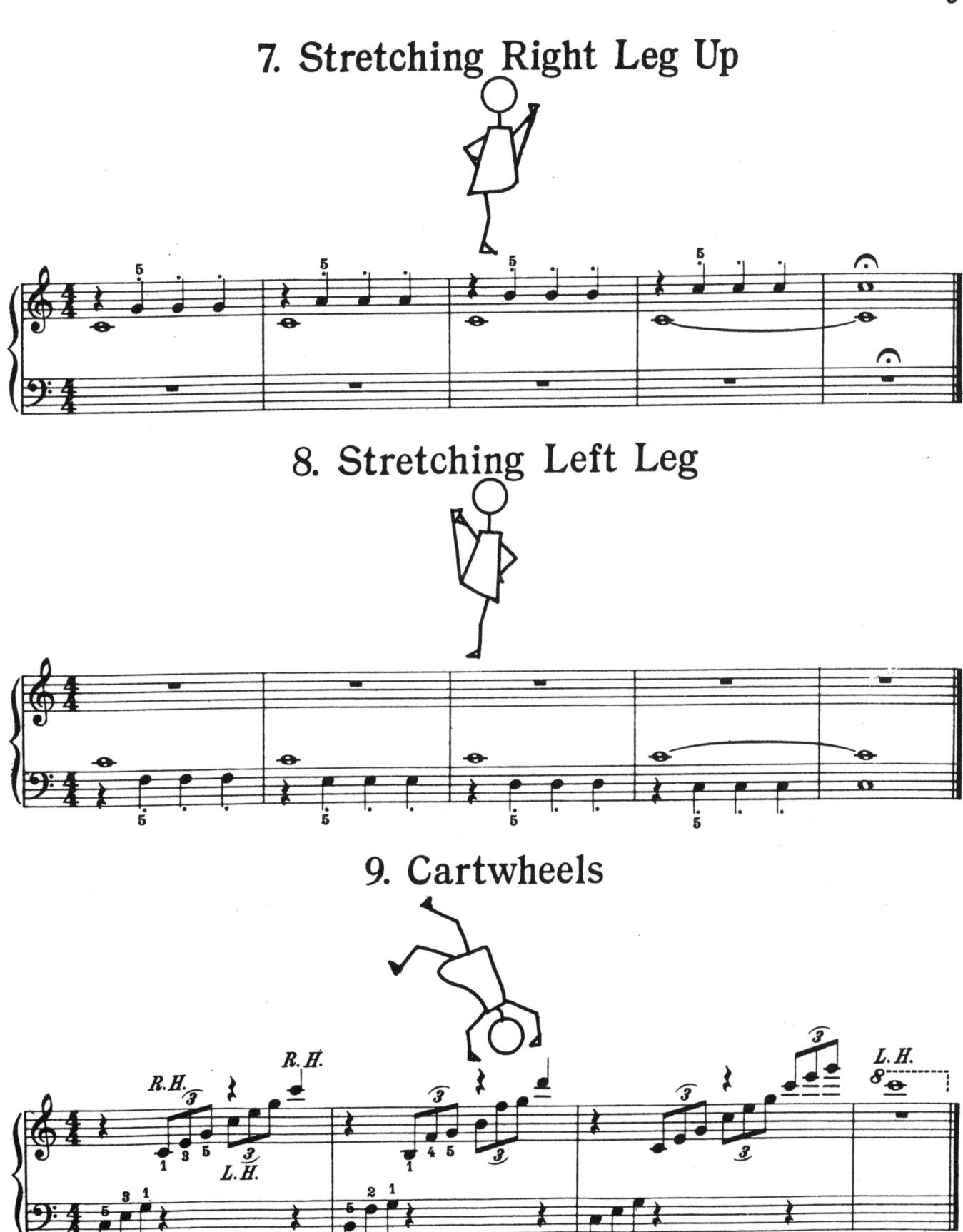

10. The Splits

11. Standing on Head

12. Fit as a Fiddle and Ready To Go

Group II
1. Morning Stretch

2. Walking

3. Running

7. Kicking Left Leg

8. The Splits

9. Leg Work (lying down)

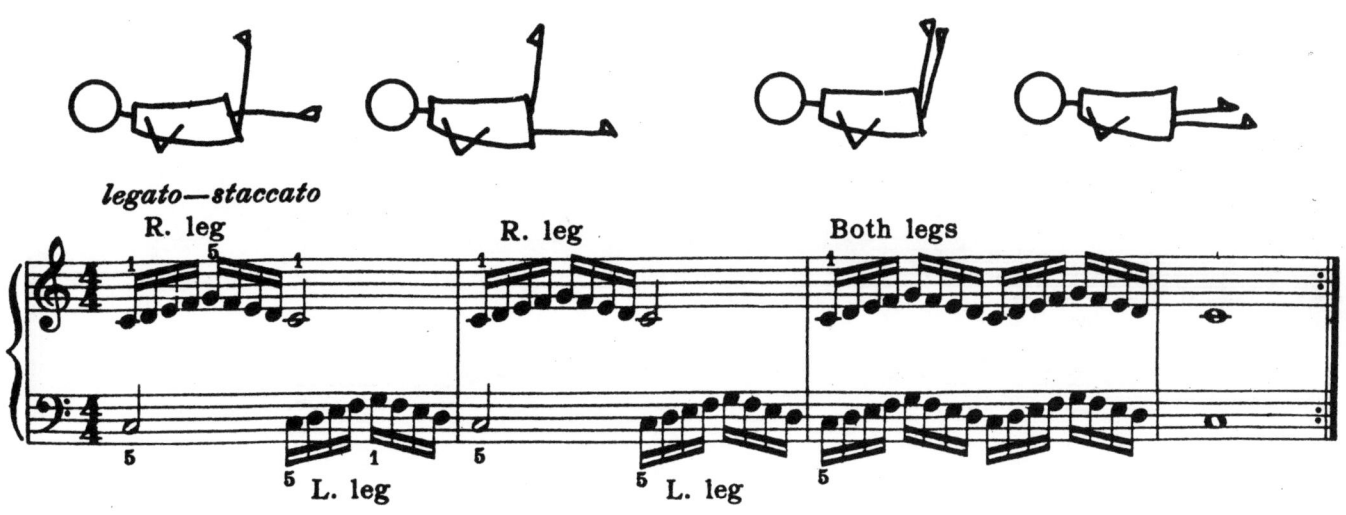

10. Sitting Up and Lying Down

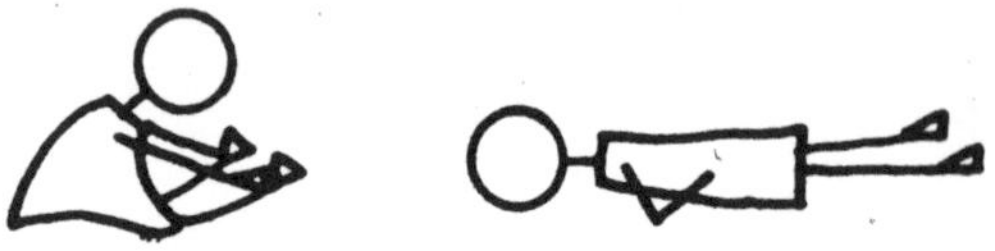

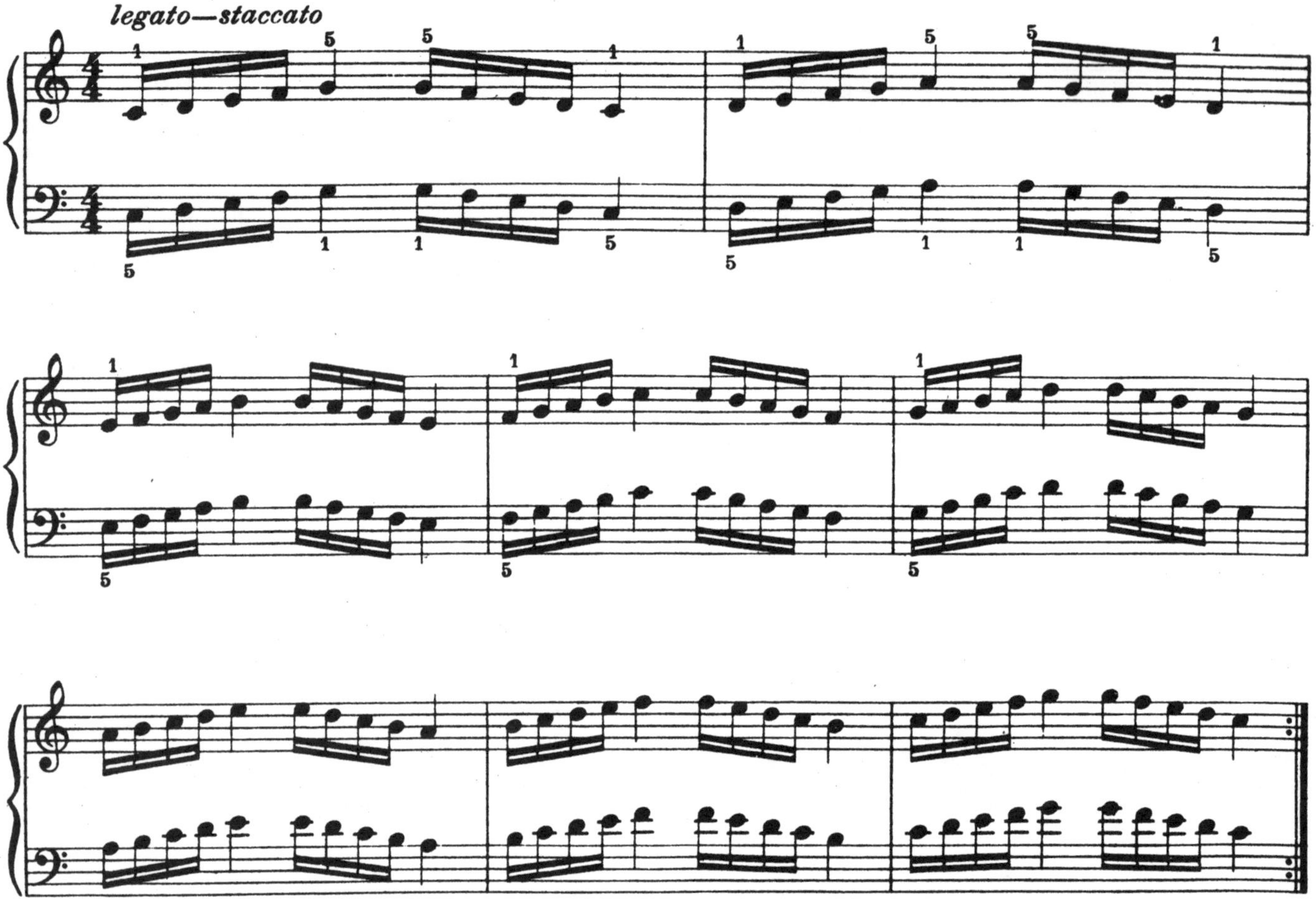

11. A Hard Trick

Practise this first:

Then practise this:

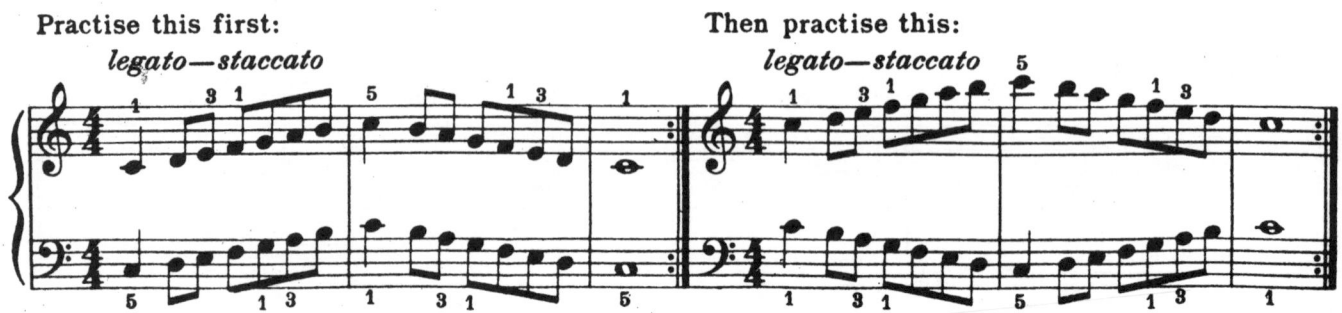

Now do the whole trick:

legato—staccato

12. Fit as a Fiddle and Ready To Go

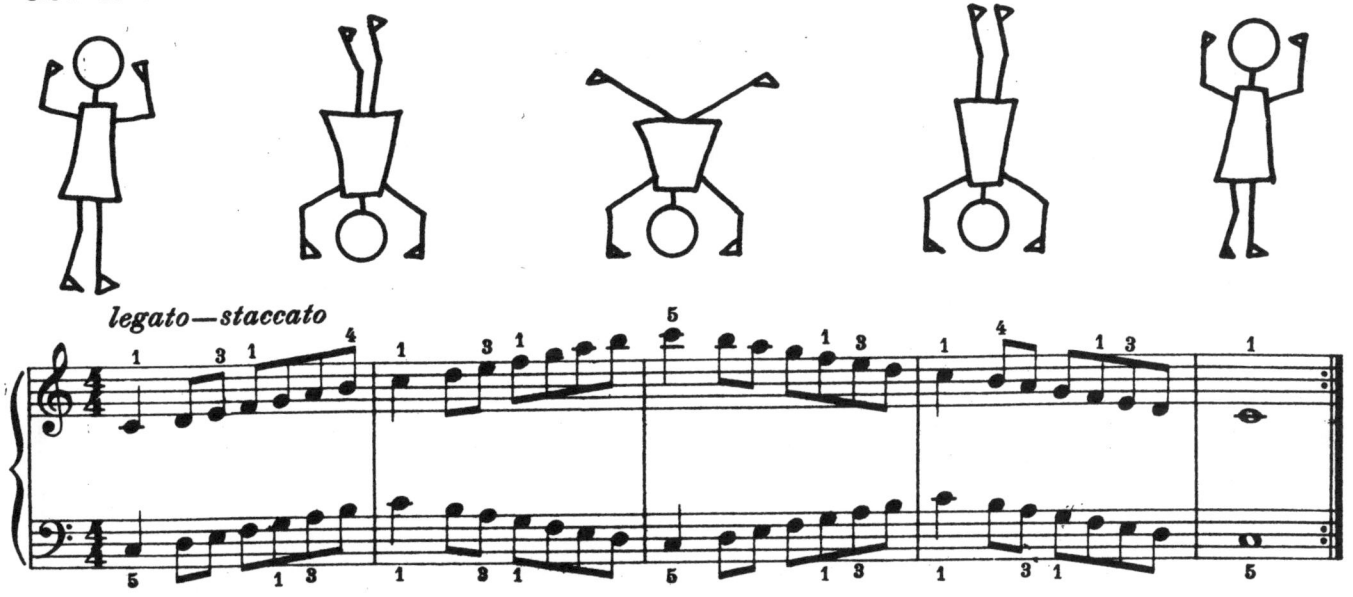

Group III
1. Deep Breathing

2. Rolling

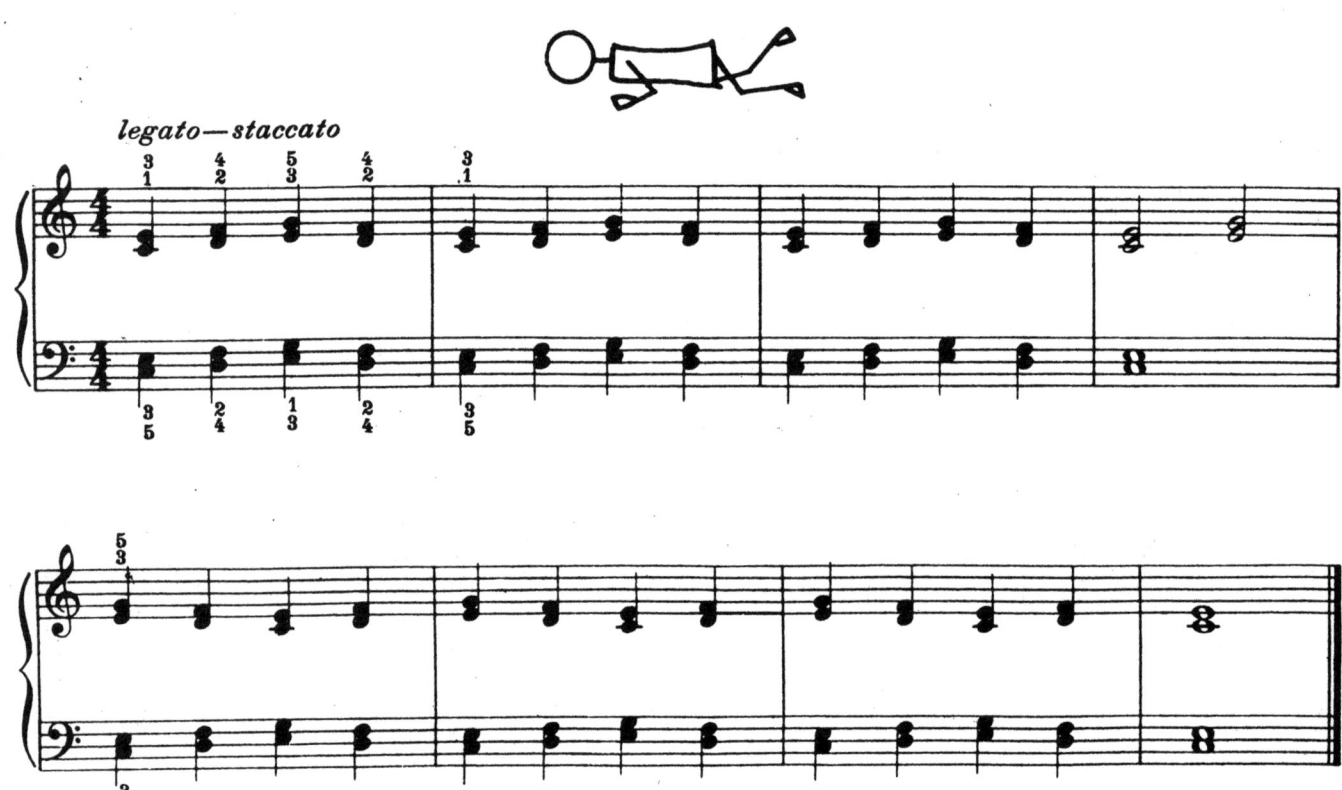

3. Climbing (in place)

4. Tip-toe Running (in place)

5. Baby Steps

6. Giant Steps

7. Jumping Rope

8. Somersaults

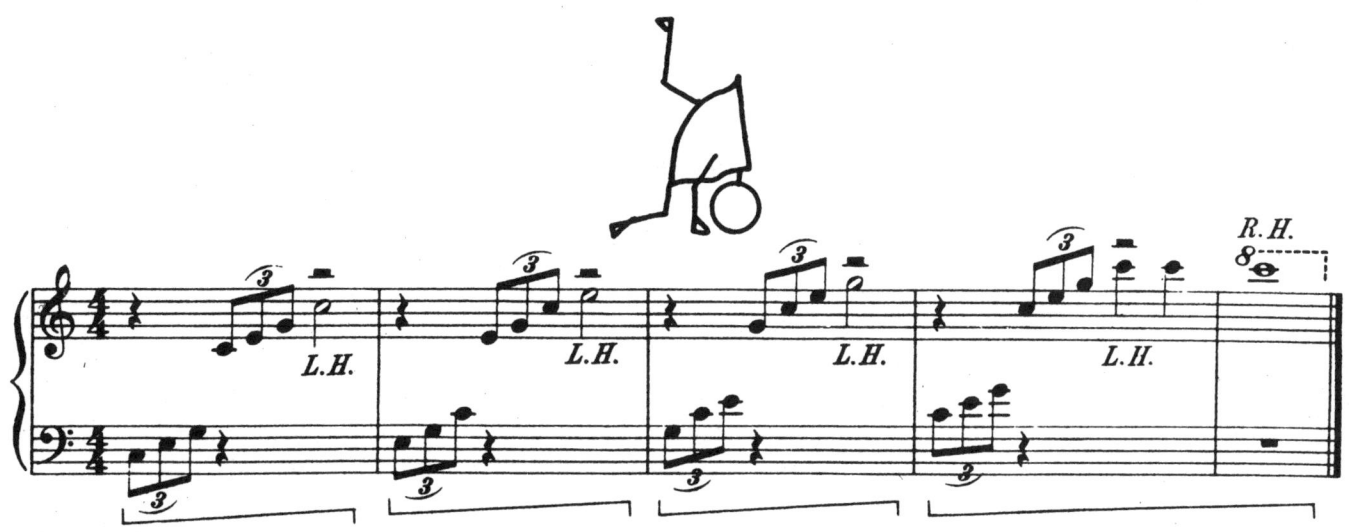

9. Touching Toes

10. Ballet Exercise ("Entre chat quatre")

11. The Splits

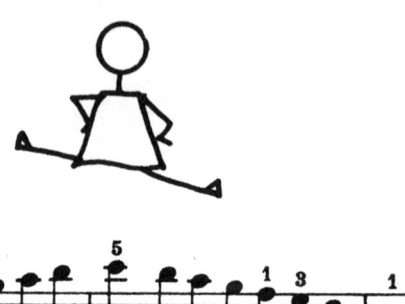

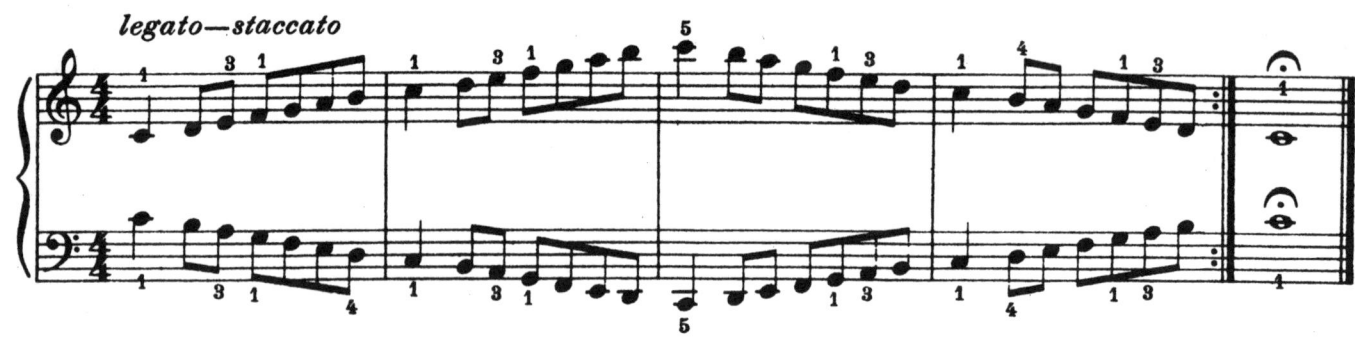

12. Fit as a Fiddle and Ready To Go

Group IV
1. Morning Stretch

2. Climbing (in place)

3. Tip-toe Running (in place)

4. Running

5. Cartwheels

6. Touching Toes

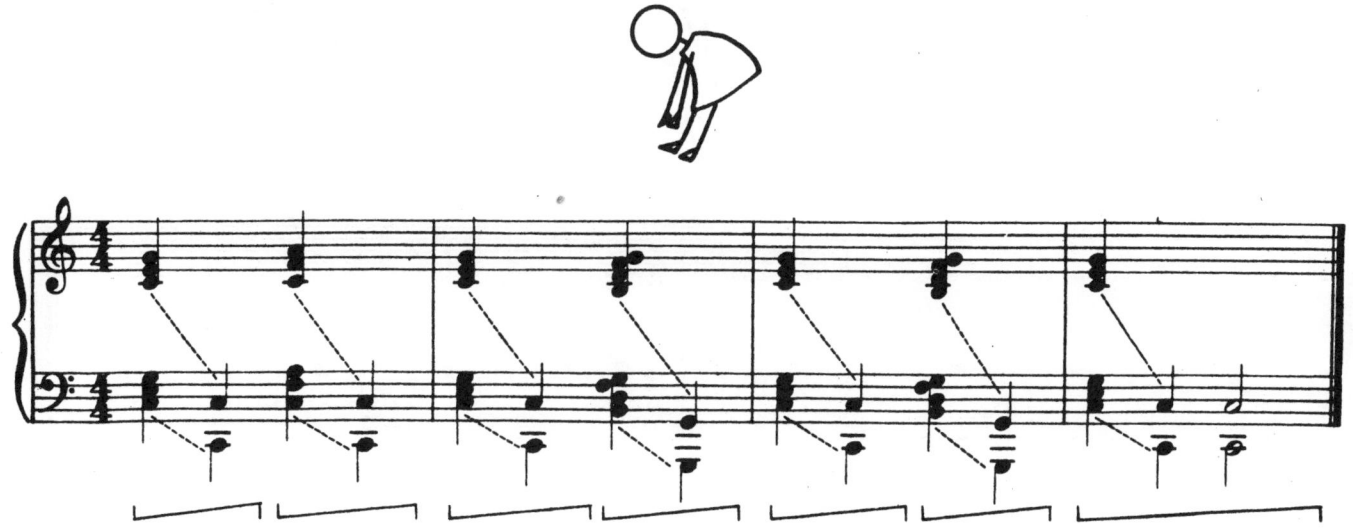

7. Hopping

8. Baby Steps

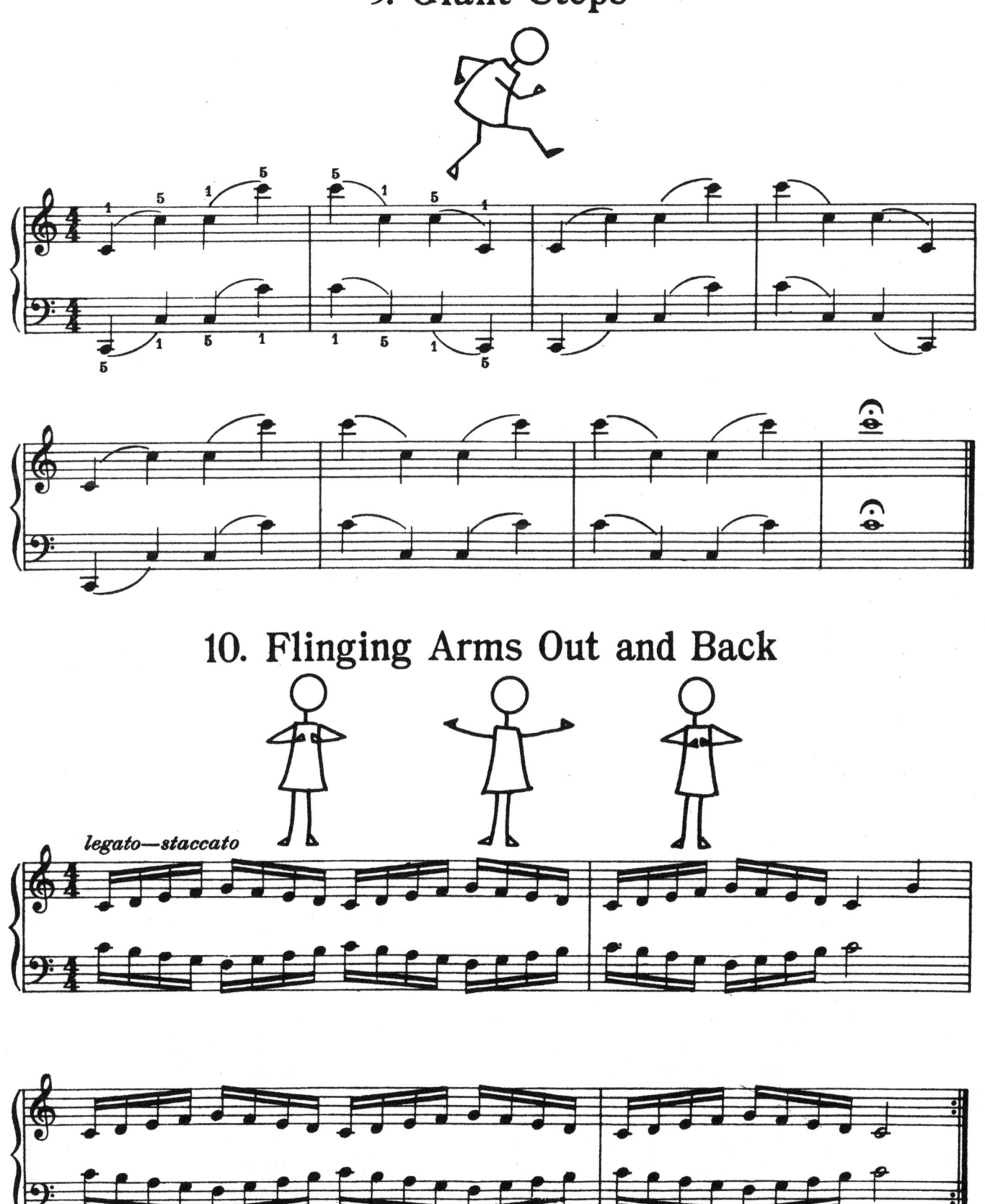

11. Standing on Head

12. Fit as a Fiddle and Ready To Go

Group V
1. Deep Breathing

2. Touching Toes

3. Hopping

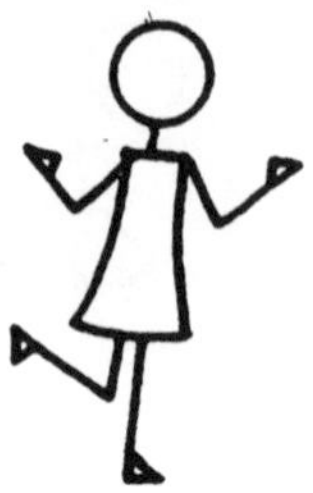

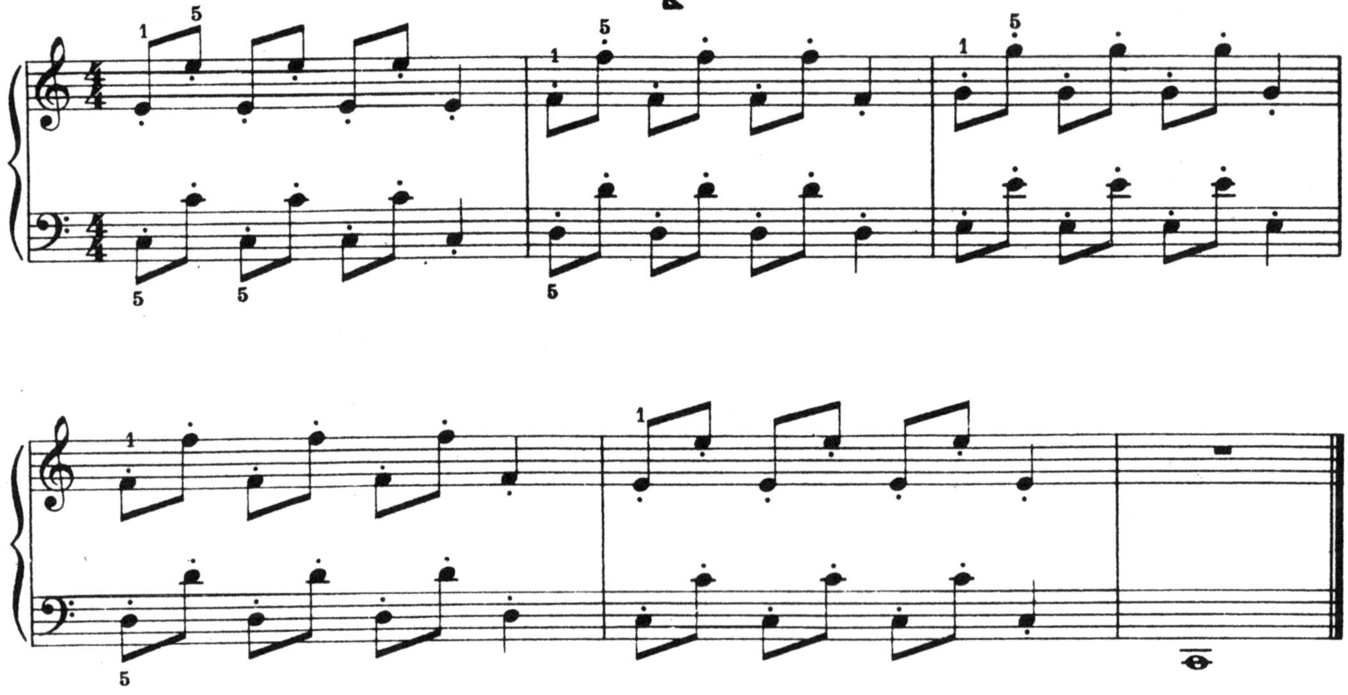

4. Climbing a Ladder

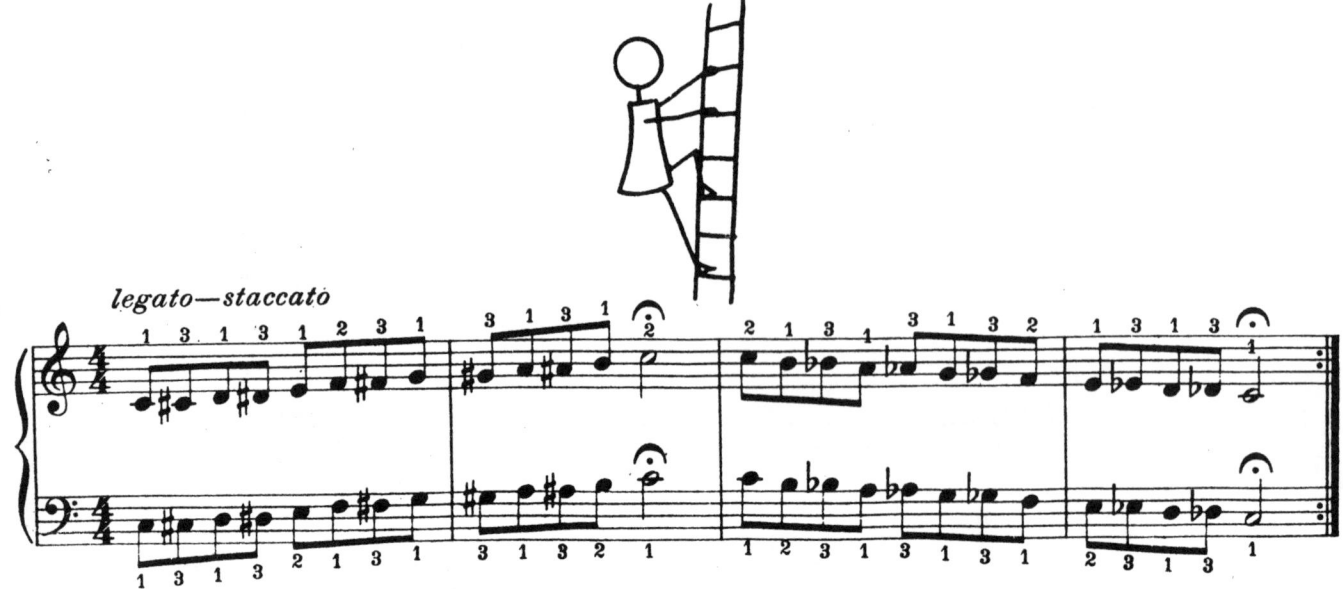

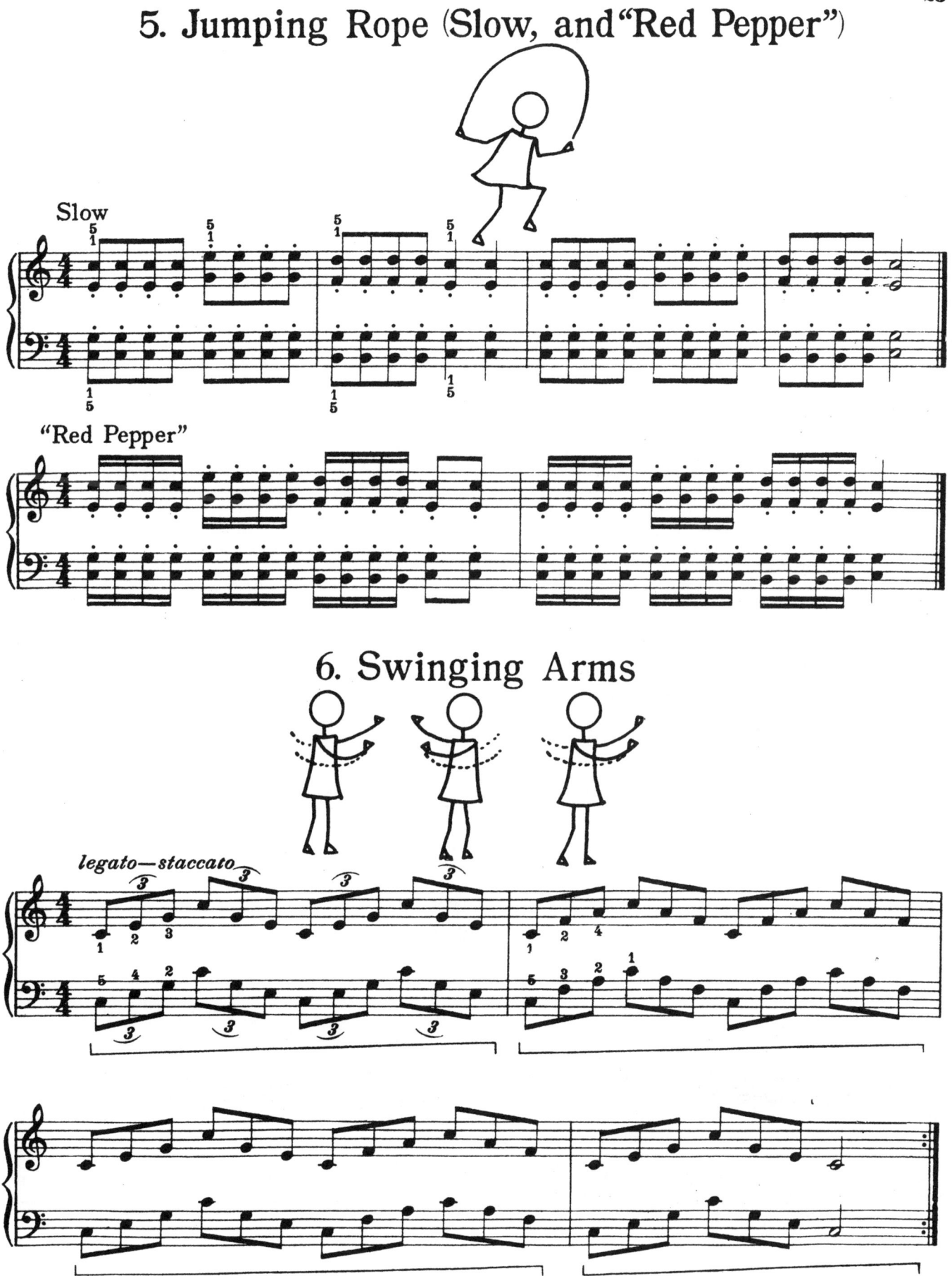

7. Hand Springs

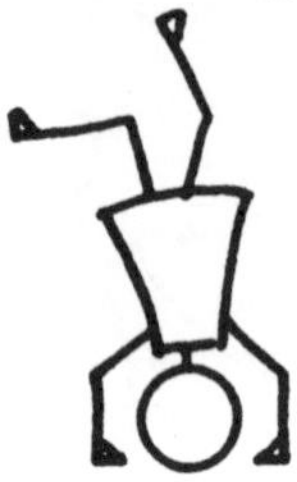

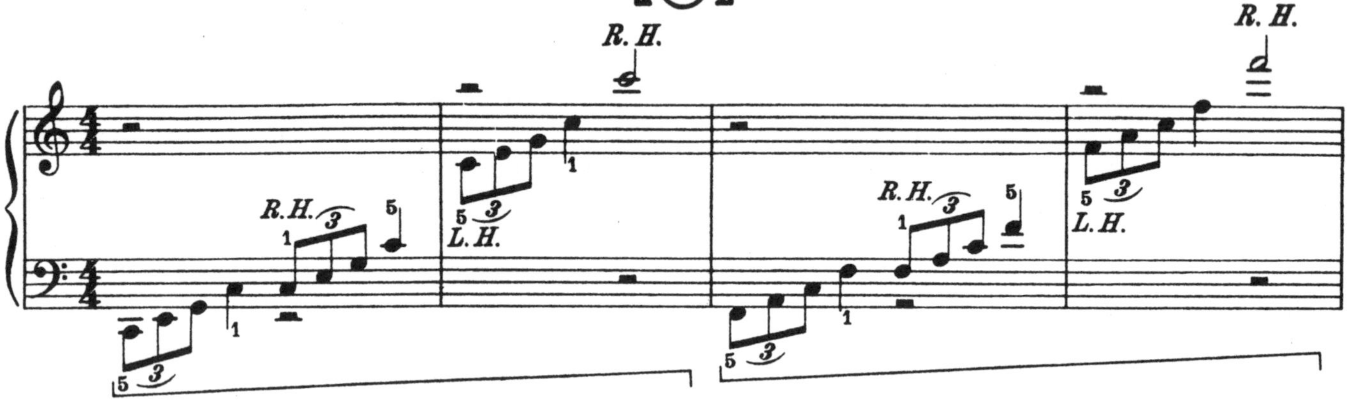

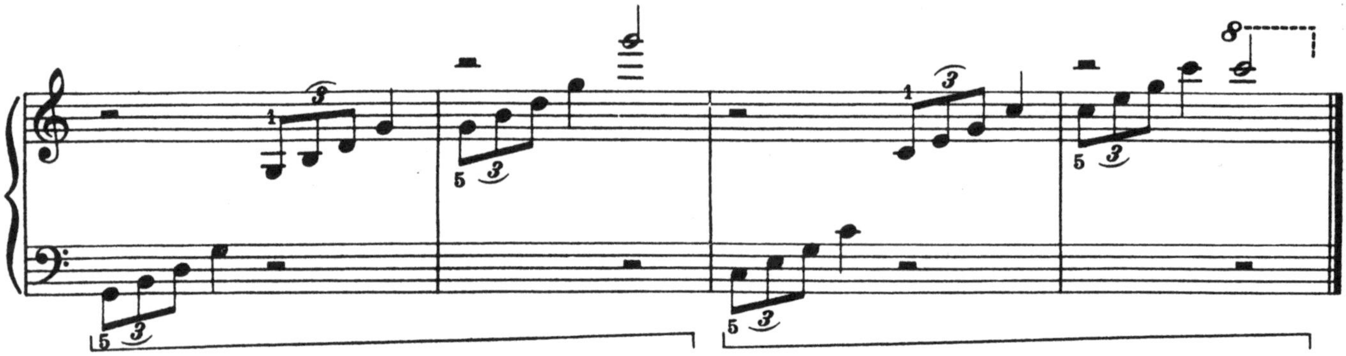

8. Walking Like a Duck

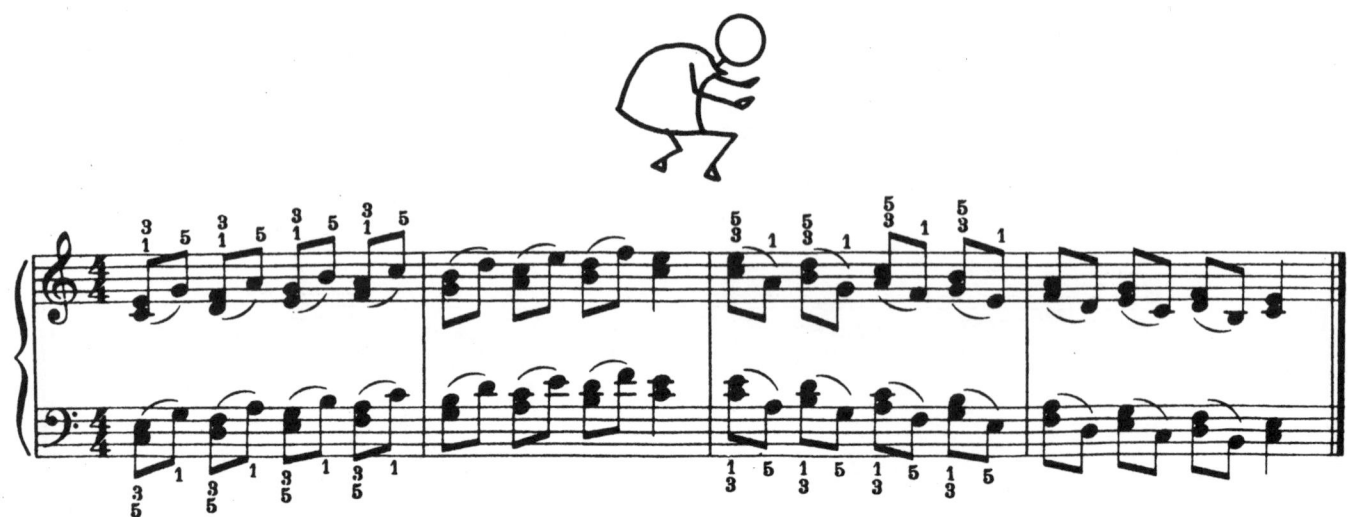

9. Bear Walk

10. Sliding Down the Bannister

11. A Hard Trick

Practise this first:

Now practise this:

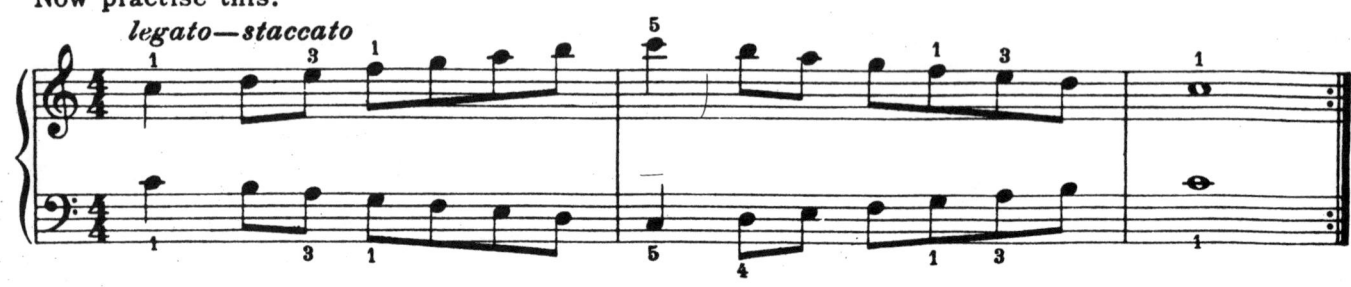

Now do the whole trick:

12. Fit as a Fiddle and Ready To Go